I0456105

Nigeria: The Way Forward

Chigor Chike

authorHOUSE®

AuthorHouse™ UK Ltd.
500 Avebury Boulevard
Central Milton Keynes, MK9 2BE
www.authorhouse.co.uk
Phone: 08001974150

© 2009 Chigor Chike. All rights reserved.

*No part of this book may be reproduced, stored in
a retrieval system, or transmitted by any means
without the written permission of the author.*

First published by AuthorHouse 10/29/2009

ISBN: 978-1-4490-3978-3 (sc)

ISBN: 978-1-4490-3978-3 (sc)

This book is printed on acid-free paper.

Preface

As Nigeria turns fifty as an Independent country, we have the opportunity to look at where we have been and where we are going. This book, the main part of which was written in 1994, contains my dreams for the country. Like many Nigerians, I have great hope for our country. But I also know it is a hope that will only be realised if we all work hard at it.

Even though I have now lived in Britain for seventeen years, I find myself with the same level of commitment to Nigeria as I had when I left in 1992. During the years I have been away, I have visited Nigeria on a number of occasions and have tried to follow events in the country through the media. This long absence will have affected my grasp of the issues in Nigeria, but it might also have given me a perspective that some would find helpful.

C C
London 2009.

Contents

1
Nigeria of my dream

Nigeria of my dream is a place where people can live happily and securely, enjoying their life with friends and loved ones: a kind and fair society where people think of others in what they do as though we were all brothers and sisters, loving and caring for each other like one family.

The care we have for each other would be the basis of everything we do. For instance, those who are put in positions of responsibility would carry out their duties with the interest of everyone at heart. Those who have opportunity would think of those who do not. Those who have been fortunate enough to make money would use it to help those who have not been so fortunate.

Our laws would be based on what is best for everybody. They would be simple to interpret and to apply. Those who disobey these laws would be given the due punishment, but also rehabilitated so as to join the rest of law abiding society. There would be order and greater regard for orderliness. There would be a societal system to everything; that is, a way of doing things that is understandable to all concerned. It would be a Nigeria where people wait their turn, patiently, due to their respect for other people and their knowledge that there is enough for everyone. It would be a Nigeria where nobody is treated as if they are above the law.

I dream of a Nigeria where it would be fun to travel to different parts of the country, travelling without the fear of accidents or armed robbers, without the irritation of being stopped by the bribe-hungry policemen or the worry that if your car breaks down you will be left helpless. I dream of a Nigeria where, whatever part of the country one travels to, one would be received like a cousin and allowed to stay for as long as one chose.

There would be less noise in the streets and less anger in the people. Streets and homes would be clean because the pride that comes with cleanliness would become second nature to most Nigerians. Refuse disposal would become a priority for governments and would be handled in an organised way. There would be less sickness; much fewer people would catch malaria and death from malaria would become rare. For those who fall ill, there would be high quality and affordable medical care for them at every level of treatment and in every part of the country, no matter how remote.

I dream of a Nigeria where people would be properly elected into decision-making positions and anybody who tries to rig elections would be rejected by Nigerians and subjected to public ridicule. Official decisions and policies would be made based on what helps and encourages Nigerians, such as what supports entrepreneurship or what rewards good citizenship, and not on what gives the people making the decision the opportunity to make money out of the situation.

I dream of a Nigeria where systemic injustice and oppression would be a thing of the past. Instead, fairness would thrive. People would know what is good for the society and they would be keen to do it. It would be a country where there is peace and harmony, where people are keen to participate in the discussion and debate of important issues and where these discussions are conducted in an atmosphere of listening and honesty.

I dream of a Nigeria where good quality education is available free of charge at all levels; a country where public transportation is comprehensive, smooth and efficient. There would be an efficient inter-state network of reliable roads and rail. Major cities in the country would have a well maintained public transportation system. Other public utilities like water, electricity, gas and telephone would be available and affordable to all. They would be so efficient and reliable that Nigerians would take them for granted, as a normal part of life.

I dream of a Nigeria where people work hard not only to provide for themselves but so the country can provide for everyone. Those who are not able to work would still be provided for. Jobs would be given on the basis of ability. Discrimination or favour on grounds of where people were born or where their parents came from will cease to be a dominant factor in official decisions. With everybody working hard, and our immense natural resources judiciously used, the economy will create the wealth used to improve life for everybody. All Nigerians would be able to afford three good meals a day and nobody would go to bed hungry. Short rest and holidays would be affordable to the vast majority of Nigerians so people are not working endlessly.

Nigerians who want to travel abroad would be able to do so without much difficulty. Many would have enough money to embark on such a journey and when they get there, they would take pride in being Nigerians. Those on business trips would readily find people from other countries who trust them to do business with them.

I dream of a Nigeria where fewer people are in prison and the prison is well maintained; a place where no prison is overcrowded. Even prisoners would be well cared for, given training in any discipline or trade they chose, so they could integrate into society when they are freed. It would be a Nigeria where nobody is forgotten in prison as "awaiting trial men", but instead where justice is dispensed quickly and fairly.

This is a dream, but it is a dream that can be achieved. What it would take is for us to enlarge our minds regarding what is possible. I can still remember debating with fellow students at the University of Benin in the 1980s who believed at the time that apartheid in South Africa would never stop. Fast forward twenty years and we have a South Africa where official discrimination has ended, reconciliation through a widely applauded Truth Commission has happened, and the country is now on its third black President.

Realising this dream would also take each one of us looking into ourselves to find out what it is we are doing wrong. What a country needs more than a good political system or good technology are dedicated men and women. There are good men and women in Nigeria, striving for change, but the challenge facing us requires more than what they alone can deliver. This challenge requires the contribution of all Nigerians. Nobody can afford to sit idly by and watch; we all suffer in some way because of the state of our country today.

2
The sense of right and wrong

It is possible to frame life in Nigeria as a battle. It is not a battle in the open but in individual lives. In virtually everything we do every day of our lives we are presented with choices. It is the accumulation of the decisions we make that form what we see as the direction of the nation. So, anybody who feels strongly about the condition of the country but is waiting for such a time when a war will be declared so he or she can come to fight should know that the war has already begun and that it is actually taking place in his or her own life.

Naturally, the choice people make about how to act depends on their understanding of right and wrong. In my experience, there has been a blurring of right and wrong in the mind of many Nigerians. To anybody who finds this difficult to believe, I would recommend the following simple exercise: Choose ten Nigerians at random and ask them whether swindling people, what we call "419", is right or wrong, and then check their answers. You may not get up to five people out of the ten condemning it.

No, our sense of right and wrong has been blurred. For instance, many people in public office no longer think that it is wrong to enrich themselves by their position, or that it is wrong to influence an official decision in favour of friends and relatives. Many Nigerians do not see it as wrong to take a position on issues purely in terms of who is concerned rather than on what principle is at stake. Many Nigerians do not appear to think that it is right to strive for fairness no matter who is concerned or the cost to oneself, or that it is wrong to think of the parts of the country as if any one part is more Nigerian than the other. We can even take examples from simple things: Many Nigerians have no regard for queuing or taking turns, unable to see that this is about respect for other people.

One's sense of right and wrong is no doubt related to the condition of the society that one lives in. In other words, people are likely to be more comfortable doing the things that they have seen other people do, or doing to other people what has been done to them at some point. But we have to get beyond excuses if we are ever going to get anywhere as a country. We are sensible beings and do not have to follow a trend, whatever it is. We can always stop and think. This is what I urge every Nigerian to do. We are all responsible for what we do. Whatever circumstances we find ourselves in we have to deal with them. Bad experiences can be turned to constructive use with imagination and goodwill. Anybody who merely passes on the wrongs done to him or her is not helping themselves or anybody else.

Every country needs people who are healthy not just physically but mentally. For us, this might require that we have to habitually reflect on past experiences to identify every hurt, pain, anger, times when we have been cheated, betrayed, denied what was rightly ours, or simply let down. We have to begin to deal with the circumstances that have led to the obstacle within us so that we can live more meaningful lives. These are heavy loads that we need to cast off. This is important because the burden of past bad experiences can contribute to confusing a person's sense of right and wrong.

But if we do not straighten out our lives and start doing the right thing, how can we continue to complain that the country is in a bad state? One may ask, if the country were your life, would it be good? Or, if the country were your family would it be good if all you did was fight or undermine your family members? If the country were your extended family, would it be good if all you did was fight and bear grudges with your relatives? If the country were your hometown, would it be good if all you did was promote destructive politics or turn villages or families against each other? If the country were a group you were involved with, would it be good if your main interest in the group was what you stand to gain?

Some people seem to find it difficult to think beyond themselves or their family. One may ask of them, if everybody left the country for you to live all alone or for you and your family, would you survive? When humans moved from a nomadic life to settle into communities, our human instinct as part of society started to develop.

It has since become fundamental to our lives as human beings that for us to continue to exist as individuals the society we are part of must exist. Anything we do which is detrimental to our society will gradually undermine the individuals within it. This is simply because we could never, as individuals, provide all that we need for a healthy life. It is based on this principle that we have doctors to care for the sick, teachers to teach the young and thereby generate knowledge, judges to arbitrate disputes, mothers and fathers to fend for the young, and leaders with all their agencies to rule and take responsibility for those things which could only be dealt with collectively.

The recognition of this relationship society and individuals within it is important for our understanding of right and wrong. Anybody who acts only in his or her narrow interest and would not contribute to the collective good of the society he or she is part of would be doing wrong. When this becomes the norm, then there is the danger that the group might collapse as a functioning society and adopt instead the jungle-principle of the strong killing the weak for food. If this were to happen to any group of people, everybody would lose out.

Conversely, good acts are those which contribute to the building up of a healthy, prosperous society. Nigerians very often throw their hands in the air in despair or use expressions like "this is Nigeria" of "the Nigerian factor" to suggest that in this place things never work smoothly or we are a people you can never totally rely on. But I do not believe that Nigerians are genetically less able to be good members of society than are any other people.

That leaves the question of where has this fuzziness in our morality come from. I suspect that the fact that public figures have never really given us good examples to follow has been a factor. There is no other choice than for each Nigerian to be the example he or she would like to see. To make any progress as a country we have to recapture the sense of right and wrong.

3
To create a just society

To put any matter in proper perspective it is sometimes necessary to look not just at the present situation but also at what has gone before and what may lie ahead. For example, if one is thinking about the future prospects of Nigeria as a country, it is helpful, I think, to look at the different generations of Nigerians.

I would look first at my generation of Nigerians. Born in the mid 1960s, our childhood was in the context of a civil war. The war affected not only Igbos like me, but many other Nigerians of my generation. Our Primary School years, after the war, saw a number of military junta's seizing power by force (or trying to), often amidst much unease, rumour, chaos and, in one case, a blood bath. Looking back, I wonder what damage television images of long lines of men being executed did to our psyche. This time was followed by the civilian period between 1979 and 1983 characterised by national name-calling and an anything-goes mentality. This was then followed by a brief period of sanity, albeit under a military-barrack style rule.

With such a childhood, being constantly aware of the shedding of blood, chaos, instability, and large scale corruption at the highest level, what kind of country would we be fairly expected to understand Nigeria to be? It might be as a consequence of this moral and political climate that in the 1990s many people of my generation turned to drug-pushing and 419. Many had formed an image of the country as a place where anything goes a place where you hit while the iron is hot, where you make hay while the sun shines. But it is also heartening that not all of us have gone this way. There are those of our generation who, with other Nigerians, are still trying to do what they know to be fair and right.

My wider point is that the socio-political and moral climate in a country shapes the coming generation. But, as always, there is a solution to this situation. There is both a national and an individual dimension to it. At the individual level, it is important that everybody think about what examples they are setting for those coming after them. This is something I myself am conscious of, as a father of four.

Men or women who habitually jump the queue at public places would be wasting their time if they then try to tell their children to respect other human beings. Men or women whose lifestyle clearly shows that they are living above their salary, or business men or business women who habitually boast about cheating business partners, would be wasting their time if they try to teach their children not to steal. In these cases, the person's actions would be contradicting his or her words. Children usually know which to believe.

How we relate to people who are younger than we are is also vital. If you oppress a younger person he or she might carry the harm of the oppression with him into the future. This would, in effect, mean that your oppressive act has acquired a lifespan longer than your own, because it lives on in somebody else. This kind of oppression can be seen at the workplace or at home and can take any form. Whatever form it takes, this must stop in order to break this evil chain whereby one generation passes on to the next all its bitterness and frustration. One example of this is when one maltreats a person of another ethnic origin because of a bad experience he or she had in the past.

As a country, we need to rethink our general attitude to children and young people. Government policies and programmes must begin to give priority to the physical and mental wellbeing of children. All children should be provided with the right environment that will enable them to turn into productive adults and responsible citizens. Every Nigerian child should be provided with good quality education that will lead him or her to a fulfilling career. There should be Government action to identity and stop all types of abuse or cruelty to children.

All of us should begin to see the children of the country as, by and large, having the same destiny. We should not be concerned only with our own children, concentrating solely on how to provide for them. Rather, we should remember that all those who are children today will live side by side in the future and with whatever injustice any of us has caused to the society. If, for instance, one child inherits a heap of money which had been stolen and set aside for him or her, as an adult he or she will have to live with the anger and frustration of those who were deprived of a means of responsible livelihood.

The only lasting provision anybody can make towards his children is to contribute, positively, to society; contribute to establish a fair and just society where talents are allowed to thrive and hard work is rewarded. Be kind to every child and think of them as the future of the country. Be conscious of younger people, bearing in mind that whatever kindness you show them they may show to others after them. These are the seeds of a just society.

4

The Culture of division

Any Nigerian who has been around for a long time will be familiar with calls to divide the country one way or another. It appears to me, whenever we have been faced with a serious problem as a country, instead of thinking hard to find the solution to it we start calling for the division of the country. It is as though we believe Nigeria should never have been created and that it can never work as a country until it is broken apart. If we add this to the constant clamour by people for states or local government areas to be divided to create new ones, one can say that within our country there is a culture of division.

I have to admit that there is something natural about this way of responding to national problems and we should not dismiss out of hand concerns about equitable representation and distribution of wealth across the country. We also have to acknowledge that there are examples of where the division of a country has brought some benefits. For example, following the break-up of the former Soviet Union, peoples such as the Ukrainians and Georgians seem to have been freed from the dominance of ethnic Russians and have gained a stronger sense of identity.

But the continuing problem with the different nationalities in that region shows that there remain difficulties. It shows that there is hardly ever a clean break when peoples and nations once have been together as one. In our case, there is no guarantee that if Nigeria were to break up into two or more parts it would accomplish anything more than transforming the current internal tensions into external conflicts between the resulting countries.

It is interesting to note that virtually all of the main sections of the country at one time or another wanted to break away from Nigeria, and this was usually when they were not holding political power. This suggests that such clamour is often motivated by narrow rather than wider interest. For some people it might be more like the woman in the famous judgement of King Solomon in the Bible, who opted that the baby in contention be divided in two rather than be given to the woman's rival. In most cases it is probably the agitator seeking his own gain rather than the gain of the country as a whole.

Something similar goes on in the requests for the creation of more states or Local Government Areas. For instance, those people who think that their town has a good chance of being made the Local Government Headquarters agitate for the creation of another Local Government area; those who believe that their town has a good chance of becoming a state capital or that they, themselves, may become more influential, agitate for a new state; on the national level, those parts of the country who feel that they are being cheated in one way or another agitate for a confederacy of secession.

But these kinds of structural changes are limited in what they can achieve and are hardly the solution we need. Our country has been split time and time again; from three regions, to four, then to twelve states then to nineteen and so on. But what this has done is really wetted the appetite for more states and caused more agitation. The tendency to see division as the solution to everything has not helped us at all; instead it has made us waste much time. Confederacy, the creation of states or other changes in structure do not create wealth, but instead divide up what already exists. If we spend all our time focusing on changes in structure and adjusting to these changes we might be neglecting other important areas of our national life. It would also mean that we spend more of our money paying public officials rather than providing for a needy population.

I believe the problem in our country is not in its structure but in us. We need to have a change of heart and approach to make this or any other structure work. We should learn to live together as brothers and sisters, not minding where people come from or what names they bear. We should begin to break down barriers between us and other people and not raise up new ones. In the same world where countries in other regions are finding new areas of cooperation and forming new alliances to make themselves stronger and to project their interest more effectively, we would be going in the wrong direction if we continue down this road of division.

This is particularly pertinent to those in leadership. They, more than other people, have to think of the state and country as having the same destiny instead of merely fighting for their own turf. It is always politically expedient to do so. What marks out good leaders is being able to see beyond one's little corner to stand for the good of all concerned. We all need to see that when everybody fights for their own gain it tends to tear the country or the state or the local government apart, but when we fight for what is right and fair to all we preserve the whole, guarantee peace and make progress. Surely, this is the right approach.

Related to our love for division is our tendency to show favouritism when discharging public functions because someone is a friend or relative, is simply known to us, or because they come from the same place or speak the same language as we do. This is also related to our tendency to form political groupings according to ethnic or language groups, or to show political support for these reasons alone.

Sadly, those in leadership often exploit these human tendencies. Sometimes they play to our insecurities by suggesting to us that we are safer supporting people like us. What I believe is that the only way to have lasting security is by working towards a society that is fair to all. This would mean individually addressing the causes of our insecurities, and whatever is making us distrust fellow Nigerians. It is important that we begin to see other Nigerians not as competitors or enemies, but as our partners in the task of nation-building.

When this spirit begins to thrive we will find that we

begin to see our multi-ethnic composition as strength and not as weakness. We will begin to see, for example, such ideas as the rotation of public office among ethnic groups as bizarre. I have, actually, once heard the suggestion that because state Governors tend to favour their home town, the solution would be to rotate the state Governorship between the different towns in the state. Considering the large number of towns in each state, you would feel really sorry for the town that would be the last to have a turn. If we take into account the fact that some State Governors favour their family members with government appointments and contracts, then we might need to have a rotation on a family basis! Our unfortunate love for shortcuts often leads us astray.

5
The national perspective

Most people thinking about Nigeria start with the country and then move to the people, who are then encouraged to contribute to its progress and think of it in whatever they do or say. A possible difficulty with this approach is that it begins with a somewhat abstract entity. To some people the approach does not work because they cannot help but think of Nigeria as the creation of European colonists. Others think of it merely as a huge bank of treasure from which they can help themselves endlessly. I do not think this approach itself is wrong; on the contrary, it is quite relevant. Perhaps the problem has been the fact that we do not have a glorious history by which to mobilize our people.

While we can see Nigeria from that top-down perspective, I prefer to see Nigeria from the bottom up; to begin by seeing people living in an area, who should be attached by their love and commitment to each other. This might sound like merely rephrasing the first approach, but I think it is more than that: this approach begins with people and moves to the country. Instead of expecting the name "Nigeria" to magically make things work, what I believe is that it is the way each person relates to the next, that is, the people we meet and talk to day after day, that come together to form the mood or spirit of the nation. This approach means that it would not be credible for anybody to habitually disrespect fellow Nigerians and yet claim an unwavering love for Nigeria.

But it is not my intention here to show the difference between my perspective and the popular approach, but to show that my approach would eventually converge with this national perspective. To start with, although I have urged every Nigerian to continue to try to better themselves, some will always be better than others. The perfect arrangement of men and women in the country would be one in which those more gifted in any given area are constantly rising through the ranks so that the topmost position is occupied by the best person.

Having now established the idea of the country as people living within existing geographical boundaries and led by good men and women, we would then begin to make progress in different areas. The ability of these leaders to see the country as one would be born of the same commitment that people have for each other within the general population. From the ability to see the country as one would come policies and programmes that are fair to everyone, no matter where they are in the country or their status in society. Their fairness would be transparent and would motivate the population to become much more productive. In other words, the goodness of these men and women would reflect back to society and reinforce the same values that brought them to their position.

In this national state of mind, all manner of desirable things would be created. The creativity, energy and resourcefulness of our people would come out more clearly. Living in goodwill and harmony, things would begin to fall into place. The noticeable gap between the country's wealth and the poverty of the people would shrink or disappear. The things we have always wanted as a country, such as well paid and motivated public workers, strong social and political institutions and a politically engaged population, but which had so far looked far-fetched would become common place. We would start to make better use of our natural resources.

Having overcome our main domestic problems, we would take our confidence into the international arena. Our activities in the international arena would not be, merely, to assert our strength over other nations, or to oppress and manipulate them as some powerful countries do sometimes, but to bring into effect those same values that had transformed our country.

In our West African sub-region for instance, our immense population and natural resources, if matched by good leadership, would put us in a good position to reach out to our sub-regional neighbours; not as a brash giant, but as a brother on equal footing in our common African experience. It would be possible for us to explore more areas of both bilateral and multilateral cooperation. In this position, more countries would call on us to help in areas where they have difficulty or to mediate in conflicts.

In the African continent, and on the world stage, our role would be similar. It would be based on these same principles of right and wrong, goodwill, harmonious living with people around you, peace within us and around us, cooperation with each other and so on.

This might look far-fetched and difficult, but the difficulty perceived by each person who reads this is really the difficulty he or she would have in his or her own life in striving toward those ideals. As I have already argued, no matter how low or high we are in society, our deeds, good or bad, affect the people around us and might influence the way those people relate with others afterwards. And these deeds between individual people are the building blocks of the kind of nation that we are and the kind of values that we can project outside our borders.

I expect some people would find some of this naïve. For their sake, let me say that I have expounded these for us to aspire to, beginning from where we are and moving towards where we want to be. What is important is that in this process we are going in the right direction. The fact that we are heading in the right direction and going as fast as we can is what we should hold on to because whether we get to our destination or not might not be entirely within our control.

6
Beyond news reporting

The Nigerian media has a duty to the country beyond news reporting. In a society still largely ignorant of their rights and responsibilities, what would be required of the media is to educate the people on these and other areas and to point the way forward. This is not to say that the media should lose balance and operate in an openly biased way. But, on the other hand, it would not be sufficient for the media to see itself as a telecom repeater station that simply receives whatever is coming and passes it on without questioning. We need a courageous and independent media able to investigate and expose corruption and wrongdoing in society, no matter who is involved. We need an active media that is able to defend our democracy, standing up for its core principles and institutions.

To perform this role, individuals of high quality are required. These would be people who have principles; people who are knowledgeable; people who are committed to the progress of the country, and have the courage to pursue good practice. What I am thinking about here are media people who have above-average personal qualities. The reason for this may not be clear to all, so let me explain by stating what, in my view, is the strategic importance of the media in a society.

The media links people together. This link could be city-wide, state-wide or nation-wide. It is through them that people are informed of what is happening in their area and enabled to decide their own course of action. The media also links the leadership to the people. This could take the form of government and citizens, the different levels in the economic community, the leadership of religious organisations with their followers. This role of forming a vertical and horizontal bridge makes the media the most influential community in shaping the culture of a people. Conversely, the change in the culture of a people over a period of time would be an indication of how well the media as a whole has performed their role.

In some key aspects of social culture, Nigeria has gone backwards since Independence. In my view, this has been, in part, because the Nigerian media has not played its role well. One example is the level to which corruption in public office has become acceptable. Another area is how acceptable it has become for Nigerian businessmen and women to cheat their foreign partners or to collude with them to swindle fellow Nigerians. Yet over this period, we have seen a boom in the number of newspapers, magazines, and radio and television stations. The boom in quantity has not been matched by an improvement in the quality of journalism.

But it would not be fair to single out the Nigerian media

or the journalists who work there for condemnation. To put the matter into better perspective, the downward trend in the quality of material mirrors some of the trends one sees in Nigerian society. Journalists like other Nigerians experience all the pressures of everyday life. They have to cater, financially, to their families and often to distant relatives as well. Like all of us, they would try to find ways to afford those things they like and to maintain a respectable lifestyle.

This situation is quite understandable. I expect that no matter where one went in the world the story would be the same. Life in this world is that of constant pressures and difficult constraints. It is no use wishing these pressures were not there. What we have to do though is choose our direction and then struggle against the odds instead of giving in to them. One cannot accomplish anything important by simply going in whatever direction the wind is blowing. And a strong and fair country cannot be built by people who behave in that way.

In the particular case of journalists, considering their strategic role, what Nigeria needs are courageous people who are prepared to make sacrifices. A journalist should be tough and capable of resisting the pressures of general society in pursuing the task of uncovering and telling the truth. He should have vision for what Nigeria can become, and this should enable him to challenge immoral activities and falsehood. This would enable him to help lift our gaze to a better tomorrow.

This is a far cry from what we have seen so far. I believe

there are many journalists who are trying very hard to do their job to a high standard, but a great majority are not trying hard enough. When a journalist takes camp with politicians and makes himself the politician's cheerleader or praise-singer, it is very destructive for the country. It is an abuse of his or her influence and opportunity. Similar to this is when a journalist adopts a cult-following stance towards the owner of his or her media house or the government (for the government-owned media houses).

I urge all Nigerian journalists (or anybody responsible for producing materials for publication) to think hard about their role to this country. Work towards cleaning up your conscience and let it lead you in your work. Remember that every time you give in to those pressures pushing you to act contrary to what you know within you to be right, you have taken our country backward and have prolonged our suffering. But when you resist those pressures, you give a new lease on life to many Nigerians and take all of us further down the right road.

I urge all Nigerian governments – be it national, state or local – to gradually remove their hands from the control of media houses. This kind of control robs the media of the ability to be objective in reporting government activities. I urge all proprietors of media houses to give greater independence to their editorial board, who should be men and women of integrity.

Let us all be guided by what we believe will benefit the country in the long term and not what will benefit us immediately. Of course, the cultural change that is required in Nigeria is so wide ranging that we should all contribute. But the media has a pivotal role in making that change, and Nigerians are crying out for better leadership within the media sector. Much as there are pressures on the media and the journalists that work there, I doubt that Nigerians have any more interest in those who have very good excuses for failing to play their role. This is why all those connected to the media should take seriously the role they have in Nigeria beyond just news reporting.

7

The search for good leadership

For a body or institution or group to make progress, it is important that it has good leadership. Let me describe what I would consider to be good leadership. Good leadership brings unity. So in the case of national leadership, leadership should be a uniting factor in Nigeria. This would require having a person who all parts of the country would find attractive. The leadership's policies and programmes would be fair and not showing favouritism to any part of the country or group of people.

Good leadership would be sensitive (and be clearly seen to be so) to the needs and feelings of the people. Whether in national, state, or local government level, for any person or group to be considered to be providing good leadership, they should be seen clearly to be responding to the demands of ordinary people.

Good leadership would be kind and not oppressive. It would be like a gentle giant, always reluctant to use its full strength. It would be wise; it would have the courage to pursue what it understands as the right course. On the other hand, it would be ready to consult widely when the need arises. It would not be ostentatious, not when many people under it live in poverty.

These are fairly difficult conditions. It would be even more difficult for anybody ruling without a mandate. Experience and common sense show that leaders are more likely to respond to the needs of their supporters or of those they feel most threatened by. For instance, military rulers are supported in power by the military. It is therefore not surprising that a military government tends to care more about those in the military. And, in my opinion, a military government will always find it difficult to give Nigeria good leadership because under this model the country will never have the link between the people and their leaders that comes from a popular mandate.

But leadership is not only to be found in government. In other areas of life, leadership is needed and these same qualities apply. Those in positions to provide any kind of leadership should be careful how they conduct themselves. Even though, in this case, their followers may not be the nation, they still model leadership to those around them. They should also instinctively think wider than their group, about other Nigerians and the peace and progress of the country.

I believe that the sentiment of division of one form or the other has often been spread by one kind of leader in the country. Sometimes it is community leaders or sectional leaders or those often termed, "leaders of thought".

This normally involves the spreading of lies or rumours about other people and their intentions. Unfortunately, the nature and extent of the upheaval this can bring is unpredictable. This wicked behaviour must stop. Any Nigerian, whether in leadership or not, who spreads a message of hatred toward one people by another should consider himself or herself as an enemy of Nigeria.

Let us now turn to leadership through national government since this is the most important form of leadership in the country. In Nigeria, the leadership we have had since Independence has not been good enough. Although there has been some achievement, in the most important areas they have failed. Without trying to analyse them one by one, the leaders we have had since Independence have failed in giving value to Nigerian citizenship. Obviously, Nigerians have a natural pride in being Nigerians. But the actions of our national leaders have taken away rather than added to that pride.

I believe that the quality of people who can provide good leadership will always be higher than that of the average person, but I also believe that the process of getting good leadership is more likely to be a gradual one in which everybody is involved – a process whereby the society as a whole is becoming better and better. The good thing about that is that the leadership will always come from the people. It means that the beautiful democratic principle of Mandate would be used in practice to choose the leadership. This selection process, which is always likely to be more peaceful than any other, would put the whole nation at ease.

I am aware that some people think differently, however. For instance, some people believe that the best way the country could make progress would be for a group of well meaning people to forcibly seize power and impose their version of good government on the people. This is likely to be a faster process, but upon close examination, the premise upon which it is based would quickly begin to shake precariously. Firstly, it assumes that this group would be capable of providing good leadership continuously without corruption. Secondly, it assumes that people would be content with a leadership that they did not take part in choosing.

Some others believe that it would not be a group but a single leader: a Messiah figure that knows all the answers and has all the necessary qualities. This, to me, is even less likely to succeed. This expectation, which is very common among Nigerians, carries the dangerous suggestion that Nigerians fold their arms and wait for the Messiah. In our present state of arbitrary morality, I doubt that we could recognise such a person even if he or she were to come.

Whatever the case, let us all be doing something while we wait. Let us, in our day to day lives, try to live according to those qualities of hard work, goodwill, peace, honesty, persistence, team work, stewardship, justice and fairness that build a better nation. Let us reject the oppression of others and with it selfishness, showiness, pettiness and wickedness that undermine the public good. This would bring a breath of fresh air to our lives and to those of our neighbourhood. It would prepare each one of us, depending on our degree of success, to take part in leadership.

8
The place of religion

In striving to redeem ourselves from our sufferings, we must face the fact that we all come with different perspectives. The different religions in the country and different political or economic ideologies that Nigerians hold mean that there is a multiplicity of approaches to both the assessment of the country's condition and the solutions on offer. I believe that in the particular task of nation-building, it is possible and necessary for us to come together, so long as what each one of us wants is the progress of the country.

Normally, religion should not have a place in the national politics of Nigeria – not as a packaged commodity. What this means is that nobody should be entitled to or solicit for political power on the grounds of what religion he or she professes. It also means that people in the country should not support candidates because of the candidate's religion. In a country like Nigeria, often teetering on the verge of religious crisis, this point can not be over-emphasised.

This is not the same as saying that religious practitioners

should not participate in politics if they chose to, or that one is not free to analyse the socio-political scene from the perspective of the religion one practices. I, for instance, try to analyse the situation in Nigerian from a Christian perspective. Some people might be alarmed at the prospect of such analysis but there is no reason to fear it, as I will now show.

What would be the Christian perspective to the problems of the country? The answer is this: even though from a Christian perspective the country is a temporal entity, its condition affects the life of the citizens not only physically, but also spiritually. A climate of corruption, poverty, disease, hunger or any other terrible evil would be a heavy spiritual burden on the individuals living within it (or associated with it) since such a climate would make it more difficult for the people to live an upright life. It means that anybody contributing to the maintenance of this unfavourable climate would be participating in the spiritual oppression of the people. Conversely, Christians who are naturally concerned about people's spiritual health cannot ignore the spiritual harm the state of the country might be doing to people in the country.

One of the central commands within Christianity is to love our neighbour. In nation-building, to the Christian, every Nigerian is a neighbour. So, as an expression of his or her Christianity, the Christian should try to love every Nigerian as he would his brother or sister. A Christian, therefore, has every reason to be a model citizen.

But this is something many of us have not lived up to.

I cannot even say that many of us are trying. There has been a growth of churches in Nigeria in the past thirty years. Last year I attended a conference in Amsterdam the main subject of which was the tremendous growth of Nigeria churches and their influence in Europe. What is perplexing is that with this growth and the new found international recognition as a world leader in Christianity, Nigeria is also known to be one of the world leaders in corruption. This can only be because many of my Christian brothers and sisters have found a way of practising Christianity that allows them to live simultaneously with corruption.

This issue is particularly pertinent for my fellow Christian ministers. We cannot continue to make our Christian ministry strictly about growing our congregation and building up church infrastructure. It is also not enough to focus on how much encouragement and blessing we can give to our own congregation. We have to be constantly challenging them to be living up to the moral tenets of Christianity. We also have to be pointing out to the wider society, including those in leadership positions, areas where they are falling down, morally. A time like this calls for Christian life that is not only about private piety but also about fighting for justice in the public sphere. We need more prophetic voices speaking out loudly against corruption in public office which is pauperising the population.

To practitioners of other religions, I advise that they should stop seeing Christianity as a threat. If what all religions are trying to do is to bring people closer to

God and to encourage people to have peace within and around them, then what is all the trouble about? If we all believe that we worship a God who loves and who would like us to love other people no matter who they are, then what is all the rancour about? If we are able to recognise good and evil in the conduct of people no matter what religion they profess, then why all the division? If we are all against the oppression and injustice taking place in our country then why can we not have more unity? If there must be competition between the different religions in Nigeria let it be a competition over who can show more love to those around them, or which religion can produce the largest number of model citizens.

The same goes to all those who believe in the saving power of one political ideology or another – such as capitalism or socialism. To some within these groups, the political ideology is a kind of religion. Although they are more entitled to use this as a rallying platform for political activity, I would like to urge that in the interest of peace they should be willing to find common ground with other Nigerians in the task of nation-building. Instead of being torn apart by dogmas, we could all come to a meeting point where we can get selfless service from each other, sincere leadership at all levels, peace and harmony in our neighbourhoods, as well as progress and prosperity. Surely, this is a desirable place for us to meet.

9
The need for social security

It is desirable to have a society that is stable. This would normally require a good amount of predictability within the society. But predictability is one thing Nigeria lacks. Socially, politically, and economically, things are constantly changing in Nigeria. Change occurs so often that you can never tell what will happen next. This is why many Nigerians find it difficult to be patient and take turns. They can never tell what drastic change is around the corner which will make them miss their turn forever. Unfortunately, every time one person acts impatiently, it further deepens the sense of instability and more people emulate the behaviour.

A way of combating this instability is to try to establish a society in which people would feel secure, a just and fair society in which the nation's wealth flows to every corner no matter who is there. A wide range of government policies and programmes would be needed to achieve this. One of these would be to establish a well funded social security system. This system would have many aspects, one of which would be to pay money to people who have no job. This would establish a safety net below which no

Nigerian could fall. It would give all Nigerians already in work a sense of security because they would know that even if they lost their job, they would be supported by the system. It would reduce the gap between the rich and the poor and thereby reduce the in-fighting in society. It would take the edge off people's desperation because they would have something to fall back on. It would create a society more at ease with itself. It might even reduce the rate of violent crimes and create a climate more conducive to business enterprise.

As part of the social security system, there would be care for those whose circumstances have made them less able to compete, such as disabled people. Disabled people would get more training and job opportunities. There would be several schemes to help disabled people work, either by providing them with the equipment they need to compensate for their disability or by the government (or its agency) subsidising their salary to make them more employable.

There would also be care for the elderly, seen in adequate pension schemes for the retired. The way many people who retire from the civil service are made to wait for years before they start receiving their benefits, years during which many of them die in penury, is nothing but a national disgrace. What we need is a pension scheme which not only covers those retired from public service but all Nigerians over the age of retirement. This would be a way of paying back the elderly for their contribution to the economy and recognising that even those who did not work for the government also made a meaningful contribution to the nation. It would be a practical way of showing that the wealth of Nigeria is for all Nigerians.

Of course, we do have a social security system at present. The various cultures within Nigeria have different ways of caring for the less privileged, either through an extended family system or through different arrangements in the community. But their success can be hit-and-miss. For example, some families or communities may have either the advantage of having more wealthy people or the disadvantage of having too many people who are no longer productive. Specific circumstances are highly divergent. There are probably many points for and against the extended family system as a social security system, but this is not the place to debate them. I would favour a shift towards a more widely operated, public funded social security system. A comparison could be made with insurance where a large number of people pool their risks together and, upon the payment of a small amount as premium, would be entitled to draw on this pool in the case of accident. The larger the number of people involved the better for policy holders and operators.

There would be issues to consider. The technology to administer nationally an efficient social security system might not exist in the country at the present time. The level of computerisation, up-to-date data and other facilities that would be required might be too great. Such a system would be open to abuse considering the high level of corruption in the country. In a country where people still get chased about the streets by tax collectors, this system might look far fetched. Funding the program might also be a problem. There may not be enough money available to establish or sustain such a system. Again, there is the economy to consider; the risk of inflation is always there.

These are all quite tenable points to consider, but I think the greatest obstacle might be us: the kind of people we are; whether we are people who care about each other or people who are only out for themselves; whether we merely pay lip-service to those at disadvantage or we are willing to give up part of our own to uplift them. In a country where state Governors readily build palatial houses to live in, annually change official cars for themselves and their colleagues in the executive committee, why can we not find money to help the most vulnerable?

Many of us, especially those in policy-making positions, need to change our attitude towards less fortunate or physically disabled people. There is a saying that it is the society that disables people: people are unable to do things because they have not been given the opportunity or the tools. A wicked society can effectively disable even able-bodied people in this way, but a kind and wise society would reach out to all its members, providing each with what they need to function until even those with the greatest physical impairments would become able and productive.

In Nigeria, we are still a long way from being a society that enables even the most physically impaired. This is to our peril because every time a person is denied the opportunity of meaningful employment, the society loses what that person might have contributed. We can slowly march towards being a society where everybody is given the opportunity to contribute. Action is needed at all levels of government in this regard. Individually, we can support organisations that care for people with all kinds of needs.

Those who think they can guarantee their security through their private arrangements might be deceiving themselves. It will always be difficult to establish a secure space to live in inside a society that is generally insecure. Let us all instead have more care for others in our country and work towards establishing a society in which everybody will feel secure. Such a society is the best guarantee of long-term individual security.

10
The way forward

I began this little book by describing what kind of country I would like Nigeria to be. In a nutshell, it would be a prosperous country where there is social justice for all and leaders are elected to govern with integrity and competence. I fundamentally believe that this is achievable. My central argument has been that if we all move forward in our individual lives in our concern for the public good, the country will move forward. Nigeria is a combination of the individuals in or around it. It can only be what we make it and can only move in the direction we are moving. Every Nigerian holds a key which can open a door to a better future for the country. Each time we make the right decision concerning things around us we open another door and inch the country forward. This is what we have to keep doing – making better individual choices and thereby taking the country forward little by little in our own way.

One of the actions we will be in a position to take is that of holding our leaders to account. Nigeria has undoubtedly had a problem of leadership. The vast majority of past and present leaders have appeared to be more concerned with using their position to make money for themselves than with serving the people. They often pay lip service to the concept of being the people's servants, but their conduct shows that they really think of themselves as the people's masters.

Bad leadership continues to let ordinary Nigerians down and to undermine our efforts to make ourselves and our country better. For example, Nigerian manufacturers and innovators are let down by government officials who prioritise importation. Hard working Nigerian civil servants are constantly demoralised by senior officials who appoint or promote their relatives and friends to high positions. Young Nigerians working hard to train in a profession have to deal with reports of top public officials who steal public funds and get away with it, suggesting that hard work is a waste of time. Hardworking doctors, nurses, teachers and other professionals have to watch as the money budgeted for improving hospitals, schools and other public infrastructure is stolen by those at the top. One could go on and on.

But this situation has thrived partly because we have not held the leaders to account. In that sense, their failure has been partly due to our collective failure. It is not likely that we will get better leaders until we start demanding better of our leaders. This calls for more commitment to the country on our part, in terms of how we live and what we are prepared to challenge. It is pointless for us to be making selfish choices in our lives and on the other hand expecting the country to improve. Whatever Nigeria is going to be comes down to what we do. Nobody is going to change Nigeria for us.

Common sense tells us to expect that many of those who are currently benefiting from the status quo will not give in to change easily. In fact, experience shows that they will fight with all they have to preserve that status quo. This is why any kind of change, especially that of a country as big and complex as Nigeria, will not be easy. It calls for much courage because the people in power may try to intimidate or eliminate those who try to make changes. But we let them succeed at our peril. One way of looking at it is that it is either we suffer the wrath of these people or we suffer the slow death of a Nigeria that is continually getting worse.

This need for courage applies to Nigerians in all walks of life. I have already discussed what it would mean for those in the media. It is hardly conceivable that Nigeria would get better as a country without a media that understands its role and performs it. I have also suggested that a government-owned media is not helpful for democracy. It gives too much power to the ruling government both in day-to-day affairs and at election time.

I have also noted what is needed from ministers of religion. Speaking specifically about Christian ministers, even though I accept that the main focus of our job (as I am a Christian minister, too) is "saving souls", we cannot close our eyes to the wrongs occurring in our society even if they are being committed by those in high political office. To close our eyes to such things would amount to giving them our tacit approval. Our role as ministers puts us in the position to act as the conscience of the country and that will involve courageously criticising corruption and political oppression.

Moving Nigeria forward calls for what is sometimes called "stickability" – the determination to stick to our course until we achieve the desired result. As I have stated, going for quick shortcuts would probably lead us astray. I do not believe there is a shortcut or a quick solution to making Nigeria a better place. What is required is constant, relentless work on everybody's part.

Nigeria is a country with great potential, but unless we apply ourselves honestly and courageously to the task of nation-building by doing some of the things I have described, that potential might never be realised. But, I am hopeful that Nigeria will not continue to under-achieve and that it will someday rise to its full potential. There are areas where we have changed, but there are changes that we still need to make. I believe that many Nigerians are prepared for change; they have seen that our current direction is heading nowhere. But we suffer from malaise, having been repeatedly let down by those in leadership and policy-making positions. It is the responsibility of us all to stop them, both by living better ourselves and by challenging them where necessary. This is what I see as the way forward.

Postscript

A practical thing we can all do would be to get together with other concerned Nigerians to form groups with the goal of pulling ideas together and planning a course of action. This applies to all Nigerians whether they are at home or abroad.

I urge Nigerians who like me are currently based abroad to not underestimate what they can contribute to the task of making Nigeria better. Following the launch of this book, I will be starting off discussions with other Nigerians to pull ideas together on practical steps forward.

About the Author

Rev Chigor Chike is a minister in the Church of England. Born in Nigeria, Rev Chike moved to Britain in 1992. He holds a number of degrees from Nigerian and British Universities, which includes a theology degree from Oxford University.

Rev Chike has been active in the social justice field in Britain for many years. In 1999 he set up an outreach project to homeless people in Birmingham and in 2002 set up a project for refugees in East London. He currently chairs a number of organisations and groups in London, including a non-governmental task group on homelessness and a race-equality organisation.

Rev Chike has published several books and articles on religious and justice issues. One of this is Voices From Slavery, which is a description of the life and beliefs of four enslaved Africans in Britain. Rev Chike currently works at a parish in East London.

He is married to Obi and they have four children, Kanayo, Adobi, Ifeoma and Chinonye.

www.ingramcontent.com/pod-product-compliance
Lightning Source LLC
Chambersburg PA
CBHW020402290526
45785CB00005B/2416